Contents

Introduction

'Perhaps, in a few years the very limited number of persons who angle in saltwater, may be considerably increased.' These words were written in 1887 by John Bickerdyke, a man of immense stature in the sport during its early years. Although obviously blessed with the gift of foresight, he could hardly have imagined a time when millions from every walk of life would be devotees of beach, rock, pier and boat fishing.

'Beachcasting' has become an art form. Casting clinics, distance competitions and even tuitional holidays have become the norm. High-tech rods and reels, the latter tuned to a point the manufacturer would hardly have thought possible, allied to new techniques, have led to the achievement of distances hitherto undreamt of. Less than a decade ago the ability to cast more than 100 yd rested with comparatively few. Today the number who can better that distance by a considerable margin, is vast.

On the debit side there is, however, growing evidence that 'distance' has become an obsession with many, who have turned their backs on actual fishing. This utterly defeats the original objective. Leaders of casting organizations must realize the danger and take steps to ensure that junior anglers in particular are encouraged to put their new-found skill to practical use, and are fully aware that fishing does not consist of hurling lead after lead on a casting field. There is a world of difference between casting to a great distance in ideal conditions on a marked out ground, and pushing out terminal tackle laden with bait, more often than not into the teeth of a fierce wind.

It's a joy to watch a true exponent send terminal rigs whistling fast and far, while the spool of a multiplier or skirted-spool reel empties in a manner that can only be described as magical.

Distance casting has come a very long way in a relatively short time, and so has equipment. My personal introduction to beachcasting, or to be more accurate, fishing with a long rod, was during World War II. The 10 ft bamboo was priced at two shillings (10p for those who know only decimalization) in a horticultural shop. It was fitted out with five rings, home-made from very stiff wire and it was, from the viewpoint of a twelve-year-old, a very handsome piece of tackle, resplendent in a coat of glossy varnish that did much to ensure that the whippings of green twine held the rings firmly in place. The rod matched with a somewhat decrepit wood centre-pin reel, which had no refinements other than the fact it turned reasonably well, was put to good use in the quest for mackerel, in those days often extremely plentiful along harbour walls and other places to which access was possible.

It was not until the late 1940s, at the age of seventeen, that I followed a well-trodden path which led to a bamboo plantation on the outskirts of Bodmin in Cornwall. After waggling several dozen bamboos of varying lengths which stood in racks along a wall, I selected one 15 ft long, at a cost of 7s 6d, which was transported home tied to the side of a car. At its butt end fluttered a piece of red rag.

Within days it was ticked out with 'real' rings with agate centres, and varnish was lovingly applied. With a basic fixed-spool reel to match, I was equipped to take my place on the golden beaches of Whitsand Bay in South East Cornwall.

I should add that from time to time, my family rented a 'bungalow' – in reality a wooden shack, one of many built into the steep cliff above the beaches. When not in use my beachcaster took its rest with others supported by brackets nailed to the outside wall of the hut. Although its only protection was a cheap lock and chain, protected from the elements by a flap of canvas, it was never molested. The memory of shouldering the weapon and making my way down a winding path to stand for hours waiting for a bass to strike at the bait, which never lay more than sixty yards away from the point of furthest wading, is still vivid.

It was not until the 1960s that professionally manufactured beach rods of 'stout green-heart' or 'whole-cane' – most far too stiff to allow a cast of any distance – began to give way to fibre-glass. The world of the beach fisherman was on the brink of a revolution.

Today, the 'in' materials are graphite, carbon and boron, and blanks are designed with great sophistication to suit different styles and terrain. On the east coast beaches, such as Pakefield and Kessingland, the best catches of cod are tied to distance and powerful rods up to 15 ft long are used. In Cornwall the demands are quite different. Anglers fishing from the vaulting cliffs of the Atlantic coast have to cast from narrow rock ledges and distance must be achieved without the aid of pendulum and similar techniques. Consequently,

the rod should be no longer than 10 ft and have a very smooth action. Tidal river fishing for such species as flounder and bass demands no more than a light- to medium-weight beach rod or a double-handed spinner.

The newcomer to beach and rock fishing would be advised to purchase a 11-12 ft fibre-glass rod with a medium-fast action capable of delivering up to 6 oz of lead. All the major manufacturers offer such a rod at a competitive price. The time to move on to the more expensive rods is when full experience has been gained. The very best tackle is no substitute for skill and a knowledge of fish behaviour and how it is affected by tidal movement. It is very often the case that an old hand, and I know more than one, still relying on a 15 ft bamboo can out-fish hands down brash new arrivals on the beach scene equipped with the best tackle money can buy.

In this book Tony Whieldon uses his considerable talent as an artist and his deep knowledge of angling to paint a most complete picture of fishing from beach or rock. He is a slave to detail, and every angler can glean much from these pages, which bring so vividly to life the world of saltwater shore fishing. On many occasions Tony has so very ably illustrated my words in feature articles published by one of Britain's principal newspapers. I was delighted, therefore, to be asked to write this introduction to his latest book, which I commend without reservation to the anglers of today and tomorrow.

Mike Millman,
Plymouth, Devon.

January 1987.

Beachcasting rods

Contoured rubber butt grip, winch reel fitting, hypalon foregrips.

Tubular rubber butt grip, hosepipe clip reel fittings, rubber foregrip.

Tubular rubber butt grip, Fuji Snaplock reel seat, rubber foregrip.

Cork butt grip, winch reel fitting, cork foregrips.

Modern beachcasters are made from glass fibre or carbon fibre blanks held together with a spigot type ferrule. Lengths vary between 10ft (3·05m) and 12ft (3·65m).

Handles can be made from the materials shown above using different permutations, if desired.

Good-quality rings are most essential in order to withstand the effect of constant line abrasion when casting or playing a heavy fish in strong surf or tide.

The serious beach angler often constructs his own rods, ensuring that the grips and reel seat are exactly positioned to suit his physique.

Hosepipe clip reel fittings can, of course, be slid up or down the blank if required.

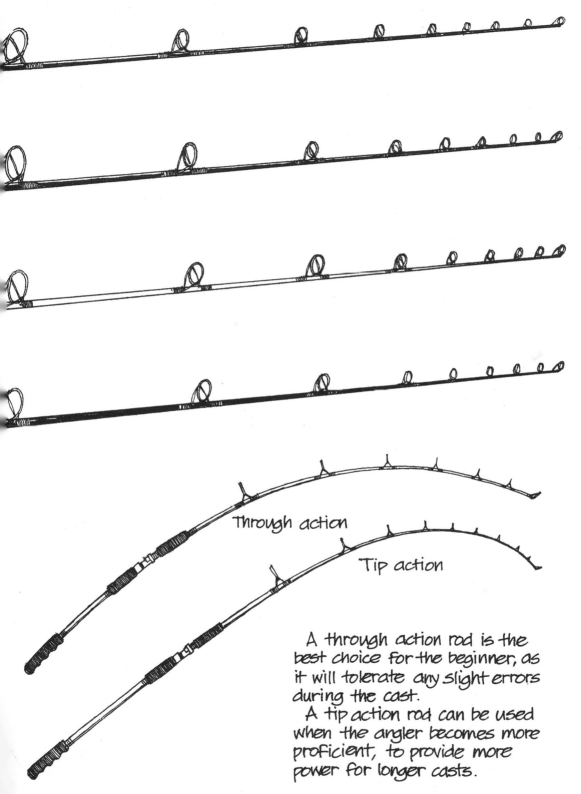

Through action

Tip action

A through action rod is the best choice for the beginner, as it will tolerate any slight errors during the cast.

A tip action rod can be used when the angler becomes more proficient, to provide more power for longer casts.

Reels

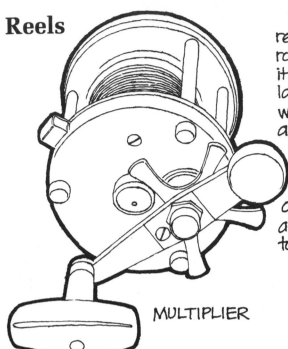

This is the most popular reel with the experts. More robust than the Fixed-spool, it is better suited to handling larger fish such as conger, or when fishing for bass from an Atlantic storm beach.

Multiplier reels with a built-in magnetic cast control system which cures overruns are now available, and are no doubt, invaluable to both novice and expert.

MULTIPLIER

The Fixed-spool reel is the ideal choice for the complete beginner. When choosing a reel of this type the following features should be looked for: large capacity spool, corrosive resistant body, and a free-rolling line roller.

Although the multiplier reel is the most popular with experts for producing the basic off-the-ground and pendulum casts, the Fixed-spool is generally preferred in conjunction with the Yarmouth back-cast.

FIXED—SPOOL

Loading a reel

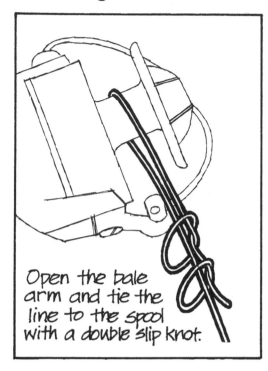

Open the bale arm and tie the line to the spool with a double slip knot.

Shock leader knot tucked against lip of spool.

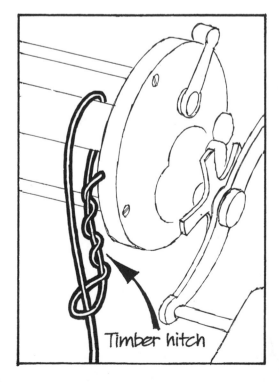

Timber hitch

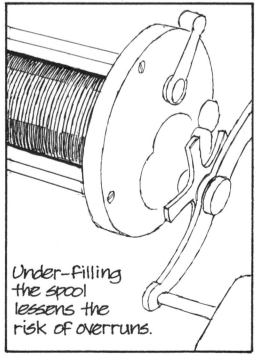

Under-filling the spool lessens the risk of overruns.

Line

14 lb (6·50 kg)
MONOFILAMENT FISHING LINE

For fishing open, sandy beaches 12lb (5·50 kg) to 15lb (6·75 kg) line should be quite adequate. Rocky venues, where conger are the quarry, will require heavier line. Good-quality monofilament line should hang limp and straight and is best purchased in bulk spool form.

A 30ft (9·10m) stronger length of line will be required between the lead and the main line to withstand the terrific tension which is exerted during the cast. This length of stronger line is called a shock leader and is especially important where other people are in the area— a lead snapping off at high speed can be as lethal as a bullet.

Shock leader strengths

30 lb (14 kg)

40 lb (18 kg)

50 lb (23 kg)

60 lb (27 kg)

3oz (90g)

4oz (120g)

5oz (150g)

6oz (180g)

To avoid injury to the thumb the shock leader knot should be tucked to one side.

Hooks

FINE WIRE ABERDEEN
This is the ideal hook for most light shore fishing where the sea-bed is clean. It is the best hook for threading on a lugworm or ragworm bait.

KIRBY LONG-SHANKED
The best hook to use when the ravenous shoals of whiting are on the feed.

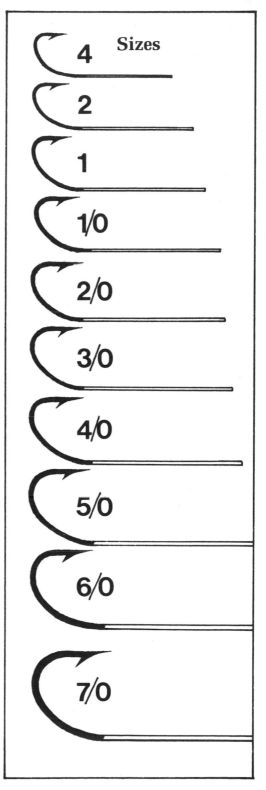

Sizes

4

2

1

1/0

2/0

3/0

4/0

5/0

6/0

7/0

O'SHAUGHNESSY FORGED
In the smaller sizes this very tough hook is suitable for bass, wrasse and small dogfish.

The larger sizes are used when a big bait is needed for conger, large bass or thornback ray.

Leads

Leads of 5oz or 6oz (150g or 180g) will provide adequate casting weight for most of the time on open beaches.

Leads of 3oz or 4oz (90g or 120g) are more suitable for fishing at closer range in quieter water. Heavy tides may demand the use of 7oz or 8oz (210g or 240g) leads.

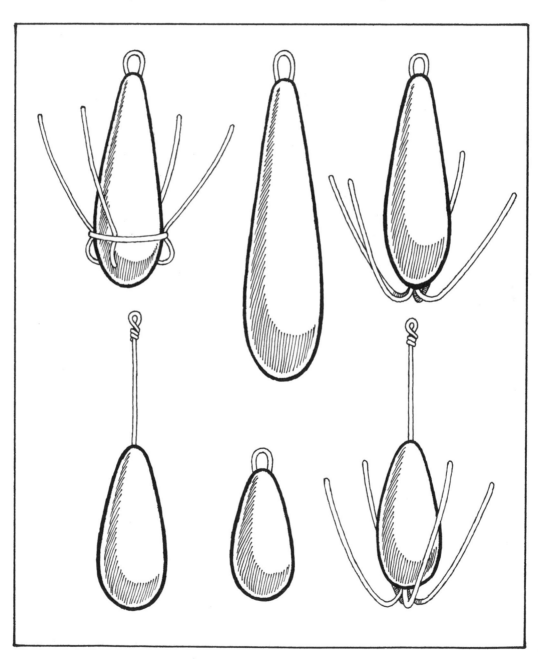

Knots

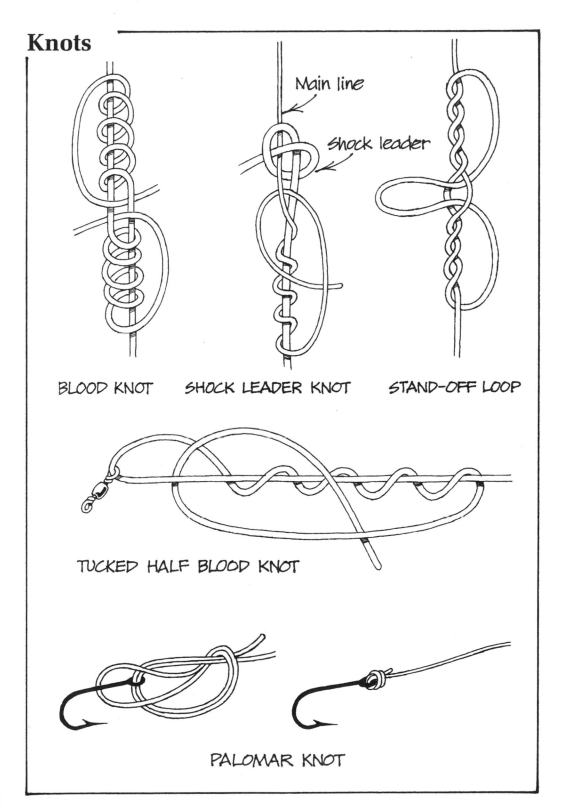

Main line

Shock leader

BLOOD KNOT   SHOCK LEADER KNOT   STAND-OFF LOOP

TUCKED HALF BLOOD KNOT

PALOMAR KNOT

Paternoster rigs

The paternoster rig is the only practical choice for long-distance casting where the sea-bed is obstruction-free.

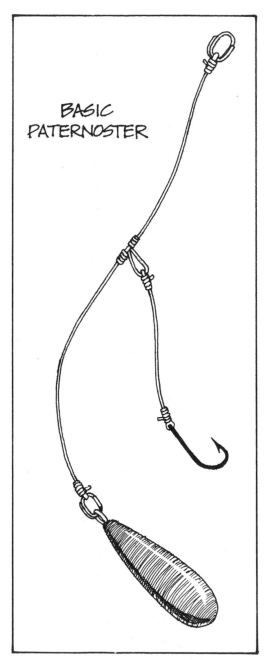

BASIC PATERNOSTER

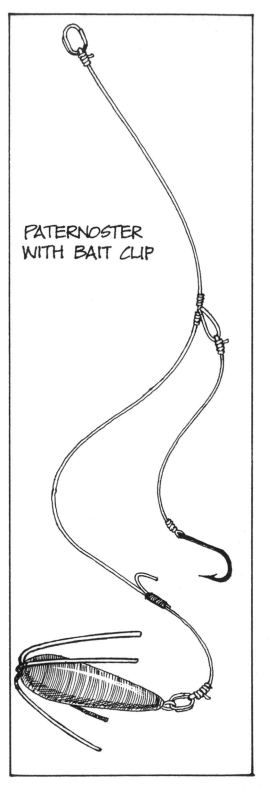

PATERNOSTER WITH BAIT CLIP

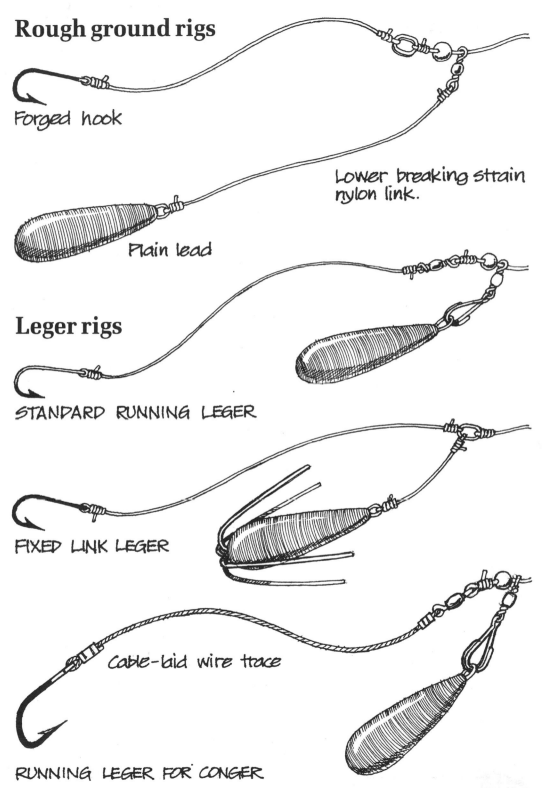

Rough ground rigs

Forged hook

Lower breaking strain nylon link.

Plain lead

Leger rigs

STANDARD RUNNING LEGER

FIXED LINK LEGER

Cable-laid wire trace

RUNNING LEGER FOR CONGER

Casting

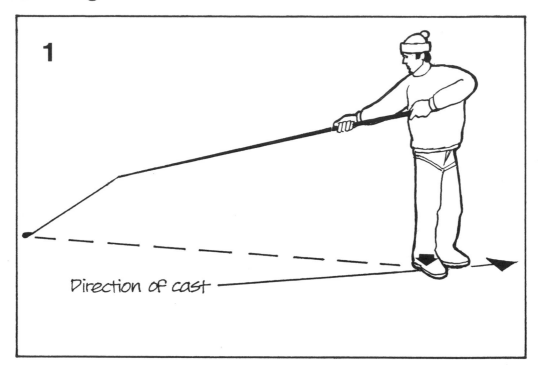

Direction of cast

Basic off-the-ground cast

① Adopt a position with the left shoulder facing in the direction of the target. Turn to the right, and with the right arm fully extended, swing the lead back so that it is lying on the ground. The body weight should be on the right foot. The reel clutch should be tightened to maximum.

② Turn the head to look towards the target. Firmly, and smoothly, pull the rod up and forward, and at the same time swivel the body around to the left.

③ As the left arm straightens, pull it down strongly, and at the same time push forward with the right arm. All the body weight should now be on the left foot.

The basic off-the-ground cast is capable of producing casts of 100 yd (91·5m) plus. Rough, steeply shelving beaches, however, tend to reduce the efficiency of the cast. To overcome this problem the pendulum swing can be used.

2

3

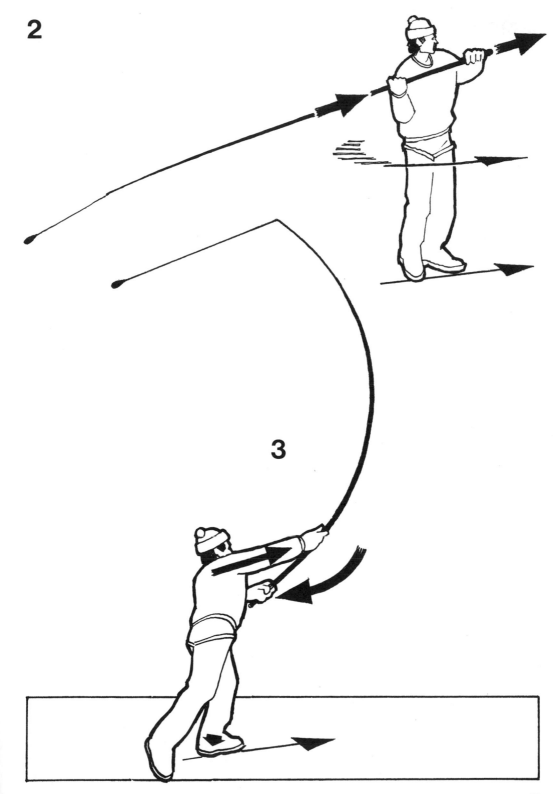

Pendulum cast

① Adopt the same position as for the off-the-ground cast, but this time hold the rod up, with about 6 ft (1·85 m) from tip to lead. (Fixed-spool reel clutches should be tightened.)

② Swing the lead to the left, then to the right.

③ At the top of the right hand swing lower the rod to the second position of the off-the-ground cast.

④ The transition from one phase to another should be one smooth, fluid movement, culminating in the power drive and follow through.

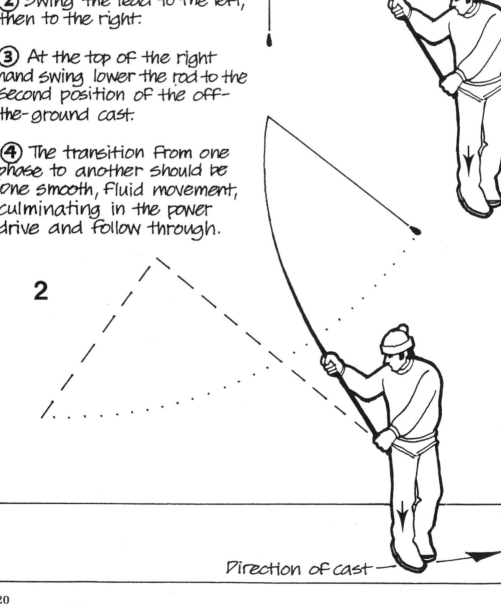

1

2

Direction of cast ——→

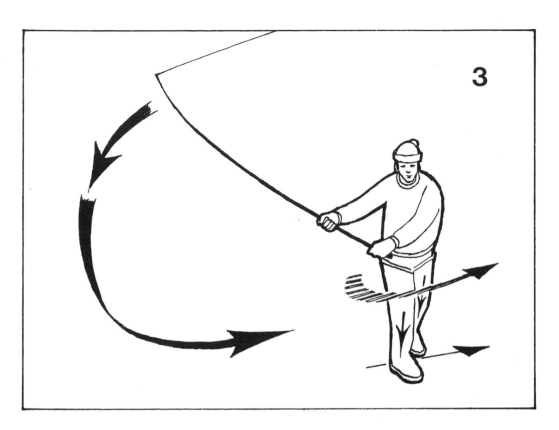

Yarmouth back-cast

YARMOUTH BACK—CASTING ROD

Strong winds, heavy seas and cross currents demand the use of heavier leads. Standard beachcasting rods will cope perfectly well with leads in the 3oz (90g) to 6oz (180g) range, but a special weapon is needed to control a weight of 7oz (210g) or 8oz (240g). The back-cast rod will need to be 15ft (4·55m) in length with a nice, easy action throughout the blank. In the hands of an expert this rod can throw a bait 200yds (183m).

Most long-distance casters cut the bale arm from a fixed-spool reel before any casting is done. This eliminates the risk of the bale arm snapping over half-way through a cast, invariably resulting in a lost lead, shock leader and terminal tackle.

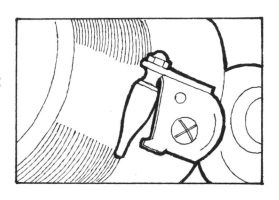

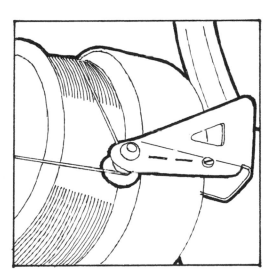

The Mitchell 498 fixed-spool beach reel has a specially-designed manual pick-up device as an integral feature.

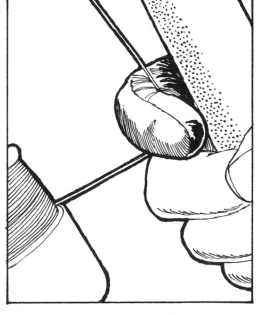

To avoid injury during the cast, the index finger should be protected with a finger stall. The clutch on the spool should also be tightened to maximum setting prior to making the cast.

Yarmouth back-cast

2 Lower the rod and push the weight forward.

1 Stand in a relaxed position and hold the rod almost upright.

3 Throw the lead away to the right and lower the rod.

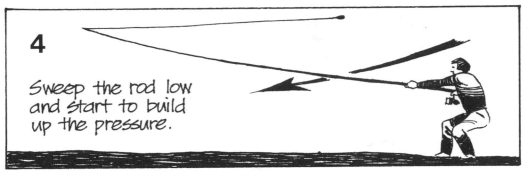

4

Sweep the rod low and start to build up the pressure.

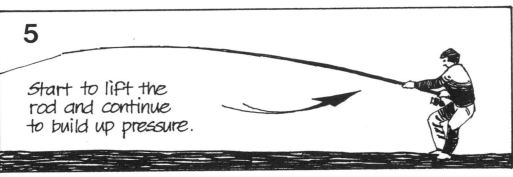

5

Start to lift the rod and continue to build up pressure.

6

Continue to build up pressure until the release— start to turn the body at this point.

7

Point the rod in the direction of the released lead.

Cast control

Even if the bale arm on a fixed-spool reel has been cut away, the pick-up should still be clicked into the open position during the cast. The forefinger is gripping the line and the spool clutch is tightened to maximum setting.

At the point of release the forefinger is straightened, allowing line to flow freely from the spool. Timing the point of release to produce long-distance casts can only come by trial and error.

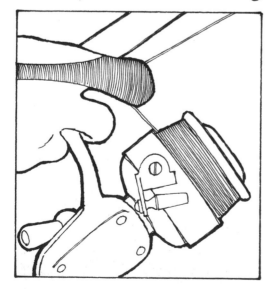

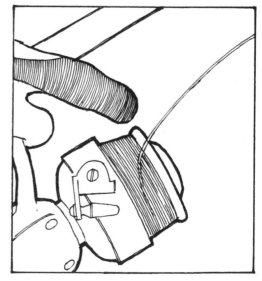

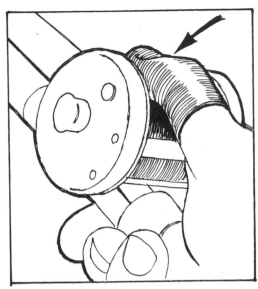

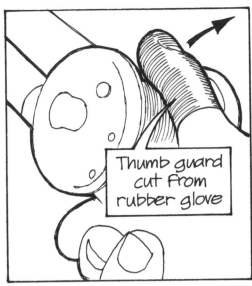

Thumb guard
cut from
rubber glove

When casting with a multiplier, the thumb should be firmly clamped down on the reel line, until the moment of release. The ratchet must be in the off position.

The line is released by lifting the thumb. Light thumb pressure may be necessary, as the lead nears the end of its aerial arc, in order to prevent an overrun.

Trouble-free casts with a multiplier can only be achieved by trial and error and tuning the reel. Most good multipliers incorporate centrifugal brakes which dampen the speed of the rotating spool during a surge. Practise in an open field or along a <u>deserted</u> beach will hopefully iron out any faults, and prepare the angler to fish with confidence.

Tuning a magnetic reel is easily done by adjusting the magnet control screw.

MAGNET CONTROL

Tides

Spring tides are high tides, and occur at new and full moon, when the gravitational pull of both sun and moon are in line with the earth.

Neap tides occur when the moon is in its first, or last quarter and the gravitational influence of the moon is tempered by the pull of the sun.

A knowledge of local tides is invaluable, not only for safety sake but for successful fishing and bait collecting.

Tide tables are available from fishing tackle shops or chandlers.

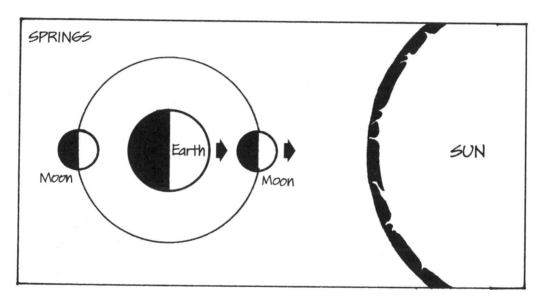

SPRINGS

Moon · Earth · Moon · SUN

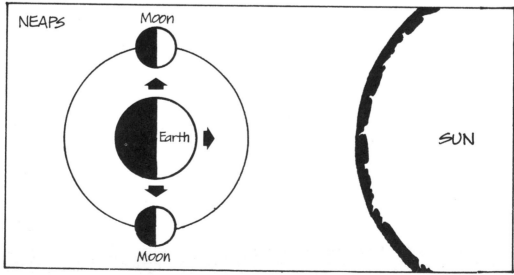

NEAPS

Moon · Earth · SUN · Moon

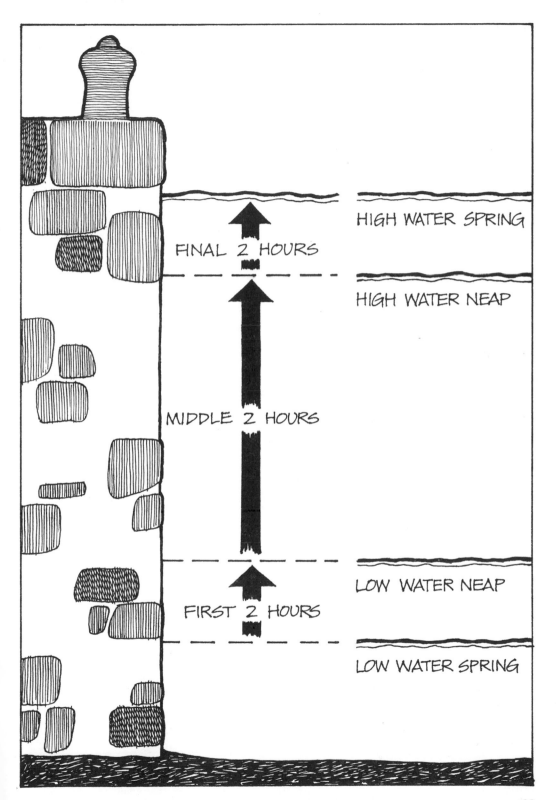

HIGH WATER SPRING

FINAL 2 HOURS

HIGH WATER NEAP

MIDDLE 2 HOURS

LOW WATER NEAP

FIRST 2 HOURS

LOW WATER SPRING

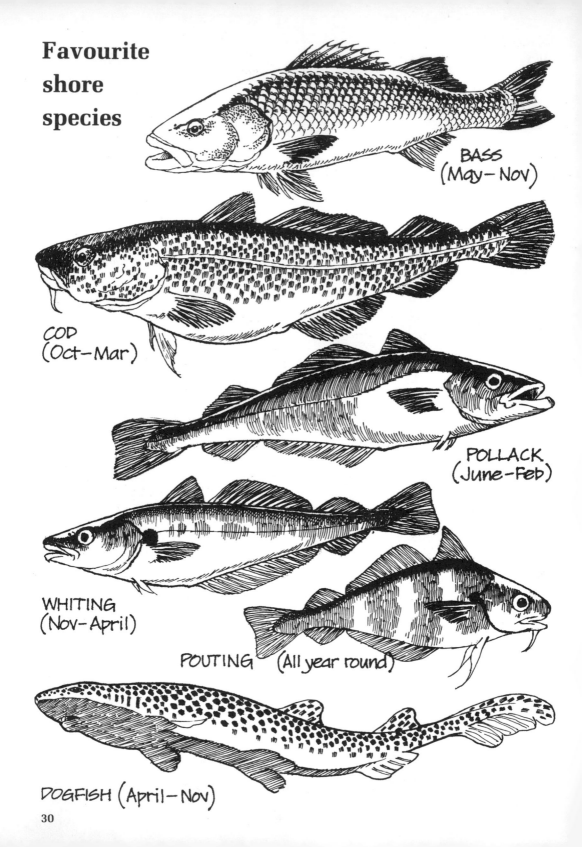

Favourite shore species

BASS (May–Nov)

COD (Oct–Mar)

POLLACK (June–Feb)

WHITING (Nov–April)

POUTING (All year round)

DOGFISH (April–Nov)

30

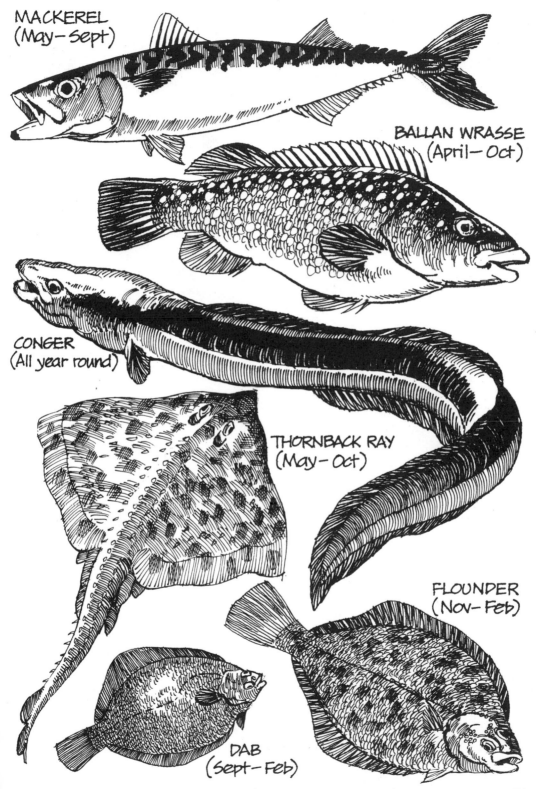

MACKEREL
(May–Sept)

BALLAN WRASSE
(April–Oct)

CONGER
(All year round)

THORNBACK RAY
(May–Oct)

FLOUNDER
(Nov–Feb)

DAB
(Sept–Feb)

Bait

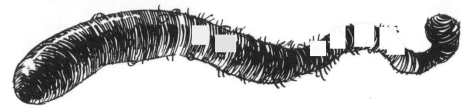

Lugworm

The lugworm lives in a 'U'-shaped burrow beneath the sand or mud. Large colonies exist on some beaches, their presence betrayed by the tell-tale casts.

Blow hole   **Cast**

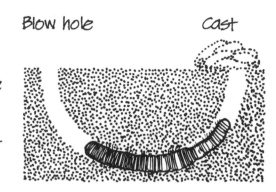

They can be kept fresh for a few days in sheets of news-paper, or for a longer period in fresh, aerated sea water.

Dig with a broad-tined fork or a spade around the blow hole and the cast.

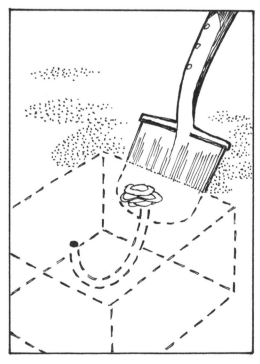

Ragworm

There are three types of ragworm used for bait.

The king ragworm is huge: one of 12in (30cm) is by no means unusual. When handling these monsters grip them immediately behind the head to prevent them turning and sinking their powerful pincers into your finger.

Harbour ragworm are very lively, reddish, and smaller than king ragworm.

White ragworm are also lively and provide a good bait for the mullet angler.

King ragworm live in a mixture of mud and shale, and extricating them with a fork is no mean physical feat. On occasions they can be exposed by simply lifting a rock.

The other two types of ragworm can be found in estuary mud at low tide.

Ragworms are hardier than lugs and can be kept for a longer period. Check daily and discard any that are dead or mutilated.

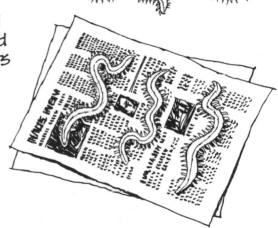

Store ragworms in newspaper or Vermiculite.

Bait

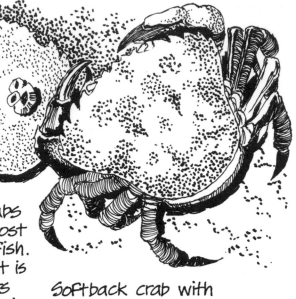

Crab

Peeler and softback crabs are the finest bait for most species of shore-caught fish. A crab is a peeler when it is in the process of losing its old shell. To test if a crab is a peeler, try lifting the rear end of the shell; it should come away easily.

Softback crab with discarded shell

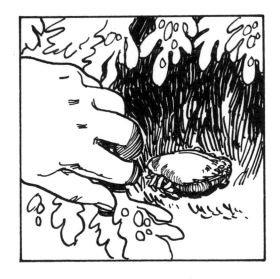

To keep crabs alive and fresh put them in a bucket or box, introduce some damp sea-weed and cover the container with an old towel which has been saturated in sea water.

When a crab has discarded its old shell it is known as a softback. During this stage it is very vulnerable to attack, and can often be found hiding beneath a larger crab. Both peelers and softbacks can be found beneath the weed on rocky foreshores. They will also bury themselves in soft sand or mud.

Bait

Whole fish

Mackerel

This is an excellent bait for many sea fish, especially the deep-water species. There are various ways of presenting it on the hook.

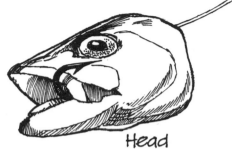

Head

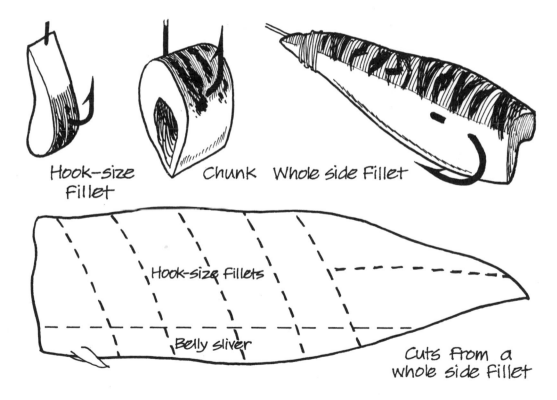

Hook-size Fillet

Chunk

Whole side Fillet

Hook-size fillets

Belly sliver

Cuts from a whole side fillet

Belly sliver

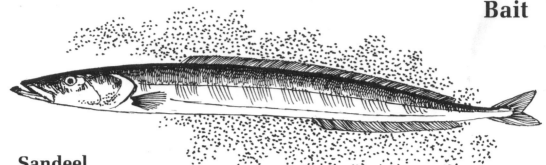

Sandeel

This excellent bait can be collected from wet sand, where it lies buried on a receding tide, or purchased from the local seine-netters. They can be used as dead bait, but are far more effective live.

Always wear thick leather gloves and thick-soled boots when digging for sandeels, as protection against the dreaded weever fish.

WEEVER

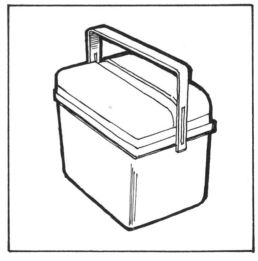

To keep them alive, store in a special bait bucket which has a battery-operated aerator to oxygenate the water.

They will also survive in an ice box. Any surplus eels can be put into a freezer and used as deadbait at a later date.

Squid

Like mackerel, squid can be mounted on the hook in various ways, to cater for different-sized fish.

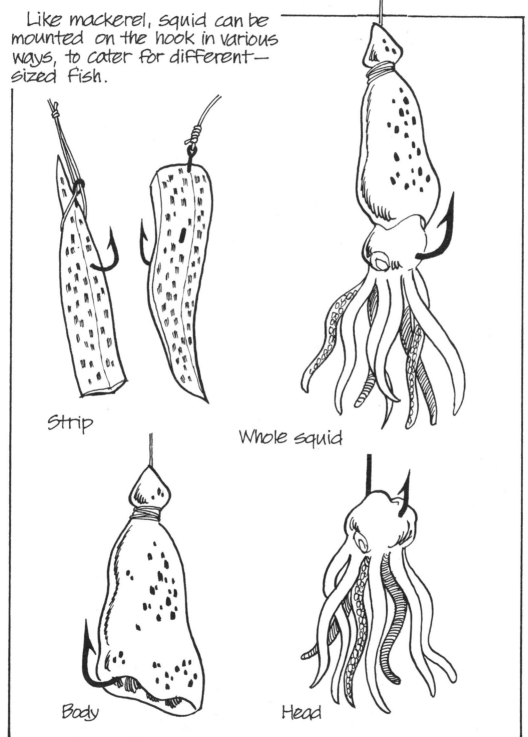

Strip

Whole squid

Body

Head

Bait presentation

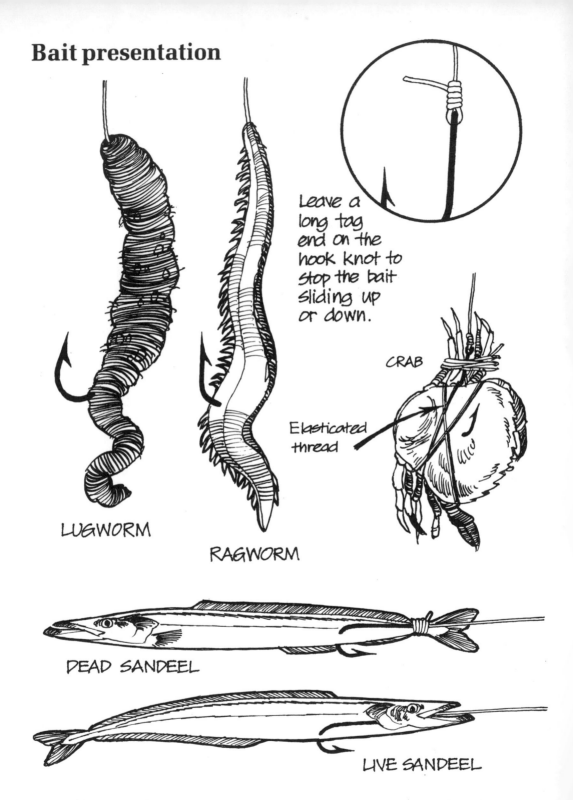

Leave a long tag end on the hook knot to stop the bait sliding up or down.

LUGWORM

RAGWORM

CRAB

Elasticated thread

DEAD SANDEEL

LIVE SANDEEL

Knots

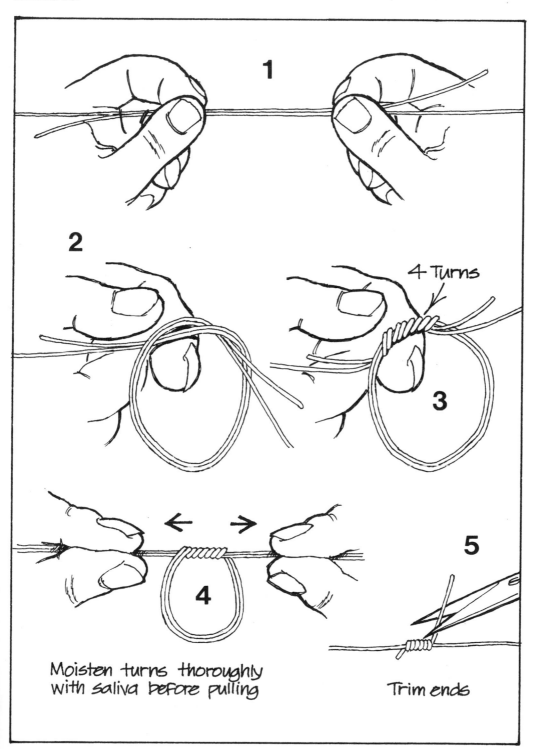

1

2

4 Turns

3

← →

4

5

Moisten turns thoroughly
with saliva before pulling

Trim ends

Fishing a storm beach

Storm beaches are exposed to the relentless pounding of the Atlantic Ocean. Long, open expanses of sand expose the angler to the brunt of westerly winds. Rank upon rank of breakers thunder across the strand and die in a table of hissing foam. At times, during settled weather, the roar of the ocean subsides, and wavelets whisper and lap where sand meets water.

However, it is the movement of the surf which dislodges and exposes food over the sandy bottom, therefore it is when the surf is running that the angler will stand a better chance of making contact with fish such as bass.

When fishing from a storm beach it is most important to wear suitable warm and waterproof clothing.

Woolly hat

Polo-neck sweater

Waxed cotton or PVC jacket with hood

Thigh or chest waders

Bass Although other types of fish can be caught from a storm beach, bass are the predominant species. During the summer and autumn these spiny buccaneers move in with the rising tide and hunt for the tasty morsels which are scoured from the sea-bed. Lugworms, crabs, razorfish and sandeels all feature on the menu.

Hotspots on a storm beach

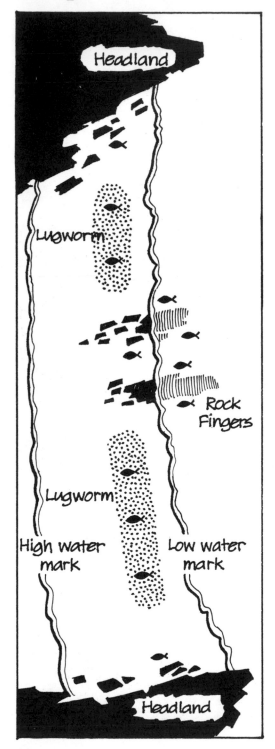

When visiting an unfamiliar beach the angler will benefit by making a reconnaissance at low tide, for this exposed area of beach will become the feeding area for the fish as the tide advances over the sand.

Alongside rock fingers are favourite feeding areas for bass, as crabs are often washed from their hiding places beneath weed or in rock crannies.

This low tide period can also be put to good use by looking for bait such as crab, lugworm, razorfish or sandeel.

Most good storm beach anglers use the multiplier reel which provides a more positive contact when working a fish back through heavy surf. The rod is held whilst waiting for a bite; the forefinger and thumb feel the line for the pull of a biting bass.

A cast just beyond the third breaker will usually make contact with feeding fish.

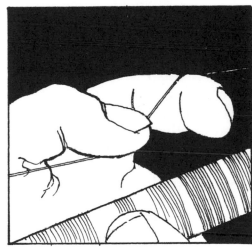

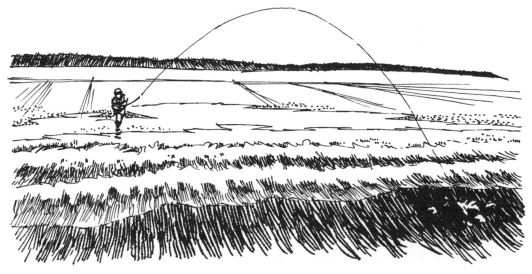

Terminal tackle for storm beach bass should be kept as simple as possible.

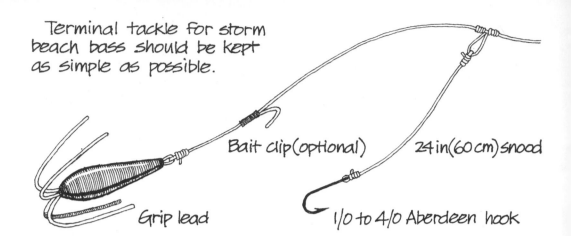

Bait clip (optional)

24 in (60 cm) snood

Grip lead

1/0 to 4/0 Aberdeen hook

A large, juicy lugworm is the ideal bait for storm beach bass, but crab will be just as deadly in areas close to fingers of rock. The hook point should be well exposed to provide positive penetration.

The inclusion of a bait clip on the terminal rig will ensure that the bait stays intact during the surge of the cast. At the end of the cast the hook will fall free of its own accord.

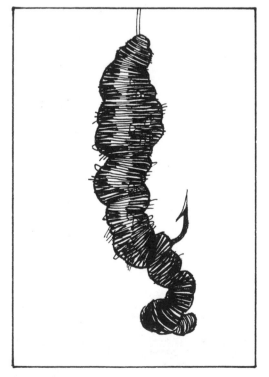

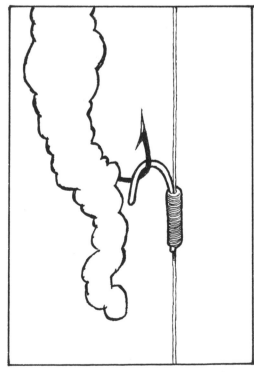

A feeding bass will usually signal his presence with one or two knocks followed by a run. Be prepared for the run and strike the moment it starts. Take a few backward steps at the same time.

When the bass shows signs of tiring, harness the power of the waves to help carry the fish closer to the shore.

Eventually a receding wave will leave the fish high-and-dry and it can be scooped up and carried clear of the water.

Wear a thick leather glove for lifting bass clear of the water to avoid injury from the fish's spines.

Storm beaches usually provide the most action when high water coincides with dawn or dusk. Night fishing can sometimes be very productive with larger than average specimens coming in closer than normal.

Always ensure that all tackle, equipment and caught fish are left well back from the water, preferably above the high water mark.

Rod rests

The monopod (A) is ideal in firm sand and mud, but is not suited to hard surfaces and very large pebbles.

The tripod (B) will cope with most surfaces and is the most sensible choice for the beginner.

The very basic but useful rest (C) is popular with many top beach anglers. It allows the rod to be propped at a variety of angles.

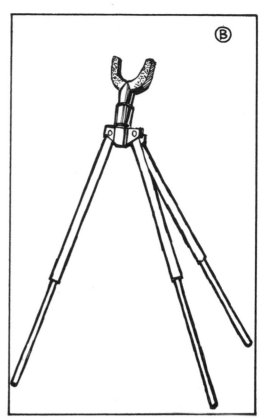

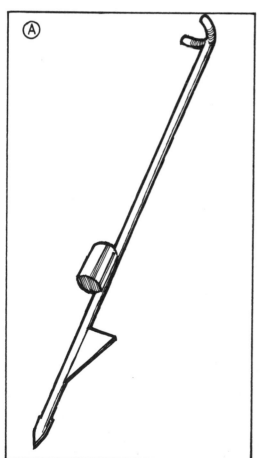

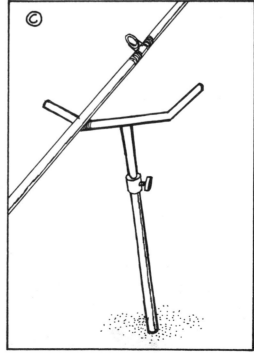

Fishing a shingle beach

Shingle beaches offer a wide variety of fish to the angler. Cod, bass, dogfish, whiting, pouting, mackerel, dabs and thornback ray can all be taken in their seasons.

During favourable conditions a standard beachcaster, multiplier reel and a 3oz(90g) to 6oz(180g) lead will cope.

Strong winds, heavy seas and cross currents will demand the use of a back-casting rod and leads of 7oz (210g) or 8oz (240g).

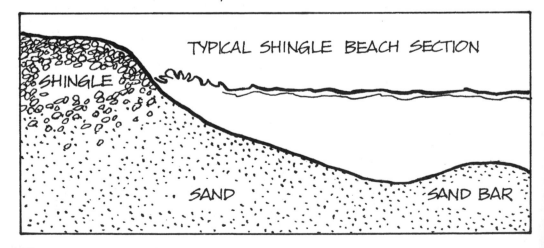

TYPICAL SHINGLE BEACH SECTION

SHINGLE

SAND

SAND BAR

Although not present all year round, cod are probably the most popular shingle beach quarry. During winter thousands of hardy anglers brave the elements, day and night, in their efforts to get to grips with a big cod.

Hotspots on a shingle beach

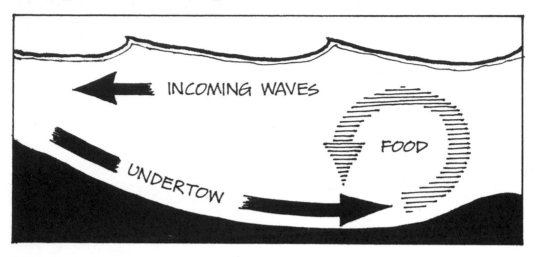

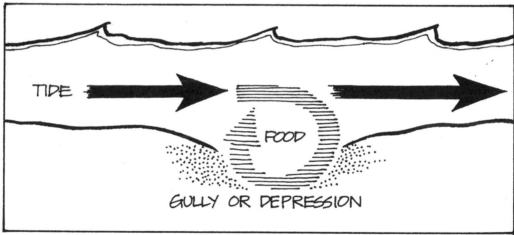

Unlike the storm beach angler, who has to leave his equipment well back from the advancing waves, the shingle beach fisherman can set up a base relatively close to the water. This is a great advantage to the winter cod angler who can prop his rod on a rest, shelter behind an umbrella, and still remain close to his rod should a bite occur.

There are a selection of rod rests available, but the type favoured by many experts is the one shown here which allows the rod to be propped at various angles.

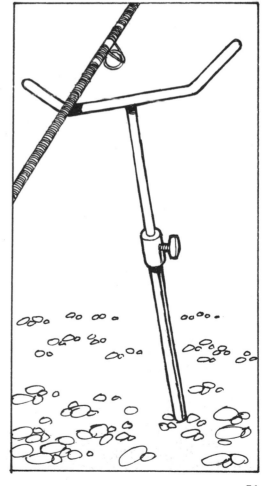

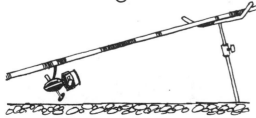

Cod

Cod feed predominantly close to the bottom, therefore a leger rig will account for the specimens.

Bead

Swivel

Link swivel

Lead

15 lb (6·80 kg) to 20 lb (9·00 kg) trace

Forged stainless hook, 4/0 to 6/0

Cod will grab just about any bait provided they are in a feeding mood — here are a few worth trying.

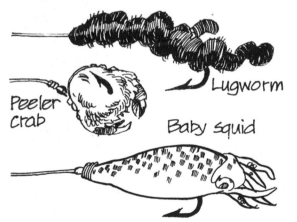

Lugworm

Peeler Crab

Baby squid

Leave the hook-point and barb completely exposed.

Plain bombs roll along the sea-bed and come to rest in depressions, presenting the bait in a hotspot.

Night Fishing usually produces the better Fish.

A head lamp is invaluable when it comes to landing a cod during darkness. This item is not very expensive and can be obtained from most good tackle shops.

Very steeply-shelving beaches may present a problem when it comes to landing a big cod. This is when a companion comes to the rescue with a strong, long-handled landing net. It is always a good policy to be in the company of another angler when beach fishing after dark.

Dogfish

Dogfish hunt in packs over a broken sea-bed. Fishing at the extremities of a shingle beach, adjacent to a rocky promontory, will often bring the best results.

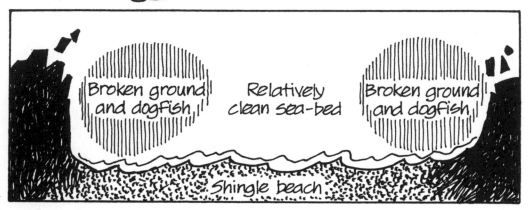

Broken ground and dogfish

Relatively clean sea-bed

Broken ground and dogfish

Shingle beach

Terminal tackle

4/0 forged stainless steel hook

30lb (14 kg) nylon trace

Bead

Split ring

Swivel

4oz (120g) lead

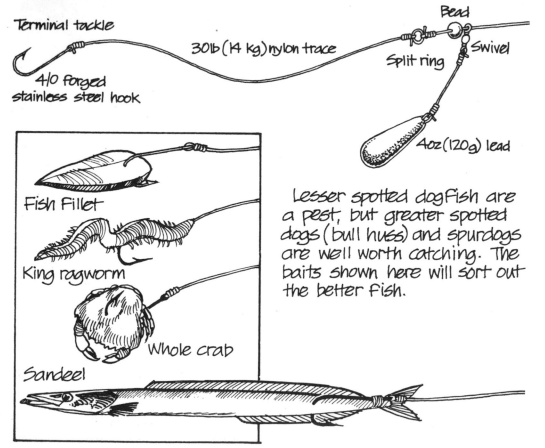

Fish Fillet

King ragworm

Whole crab

Sandeel

Lesser spotted dogfish are a pest, but greater spotted dogs (bull huss) and spurdogs are well worth catching. The baits shown here will sort out the better fish.

Whiting

The best time to pursue this ravenous fish is at night, when it is possible to take fish in quick succession. During the winter they come close inshore and can be caught from all shingle beaches.

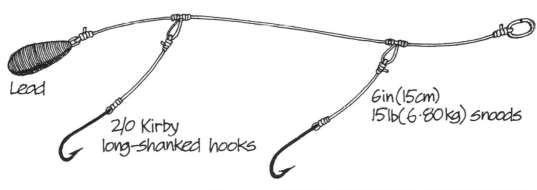

Lead

2/0 Kirby long-shanked hooks

6in(15cm) 15lb(6·80kg) snoods

BAITS

Mackerel or herring chunk

Lugworm/fish cocktail

Lugworm

Pouting

Like the whiting, the pouting feeds more freely after dark and will take any bait that is offered.

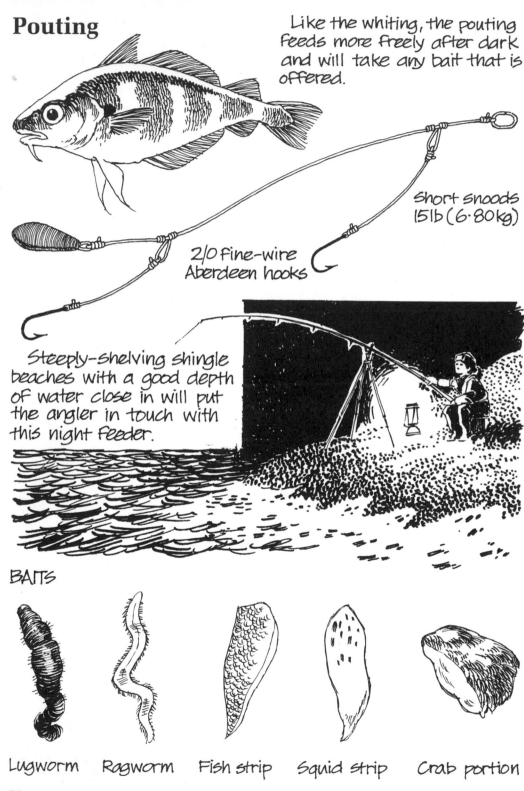

Short snoods
15lb (6·80kg)

2/0 fine-wire
Aberdeen hooks

Steeply-shelving shingle beaches with a good depth of water close in will put the angler in touch with this night feeder.

BAITS

Lugworm   Ragworm   Fish strip   Squid strip   Crab portion

Mackerel

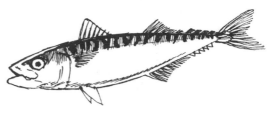

During the summer months mackerel chase small fry very close to the shoreline. Steeply-shelving beaches with a good depth of water will bring these predators within casting range of the angler.

A beachcasting rod is ideally suited to casting a team of feathers amongst the feeding mackerel.

3oz–4oz (90g–120g) Lead

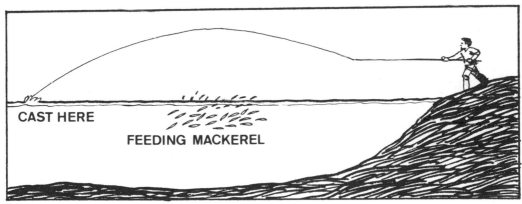

CAST HERE

FEEDING MACKEREL

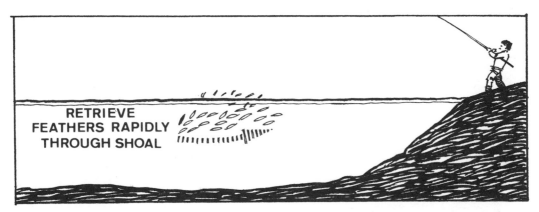

RETRIEVE FEATHERS RAPIDLY THROUGH SHOAL

Dabs

These are delightful little fish. They bite boldly and make excellent eating. Their favourite feeding grounds are over beds of hard-packed sand and shingle.

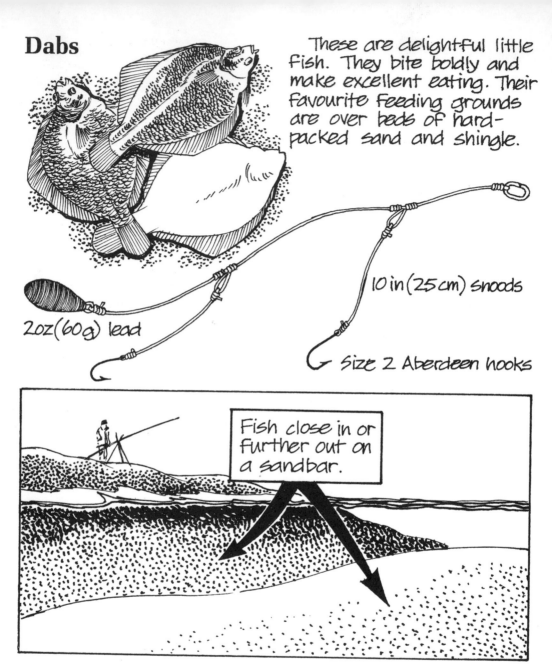

2oz (60g) lead

10 in (25cm) snoods

Size 2 Aberdeen hooks

Fish close in or further out on a sandbar.

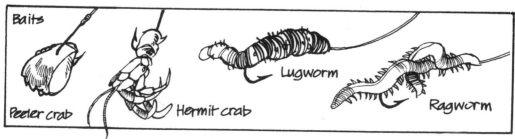

Baits

Peeler crab

Hermit crab

Lugworm

Ragworm

Thornback ray

A warm summer evening with a rising tide is the ideal combination for taking this bottom feeder.

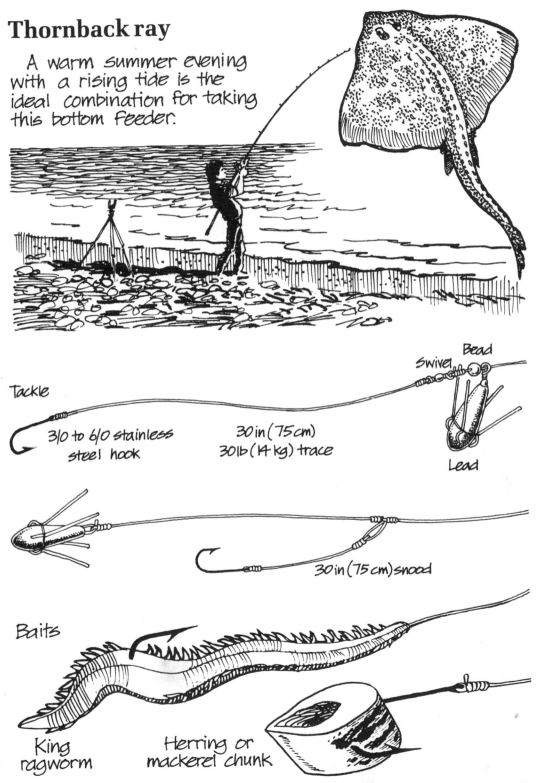

Tackle

3/0 to 6/0 stainless steel hook

30 in (75 cm)
30 lb (14 kg) trace

Swivel

Bead

Lead

30 in (75 cm) snood

Baits

King ragworm

Herring or mackerel chunk

Fishing from rocks

Rocks provide a haven for small creatures. Prawns, small fish, crabs and shellfish all shelter in the crevices and under the weed. These creatures form the diet of fish such as bass, conger, pollack and wrasse. As the tide flows and the water level creeps higher over the rocks food is flushed out and the predators feed.

A standard beachcasting rod is the ideal tool for rock fishing as the extra length permits more control over a hooked fish. It is advisable to step up the breaking strain of the main line when fishing rocky areas — abrasion from underwater rocks could result in a lost fish. However, lead links are best constructed of a lower breaking strain monofilament which will snap, under pressure, should the lead become snagged in a rock crevice. The main bulk of the terminal rig can then be retrieved intact. Where lead losses are high, old spark plugs can be used as a substitute weight.

There is seldom need to cast far from rocks – fish can often be caught directly beneath the rod tip.

As a safety precaution the angler should make sure that, at all stages of the tide, there is a way of exit to safe ground. It is also a good policy to inform a friend or relative of your fishing position and the time that you intend to return home.

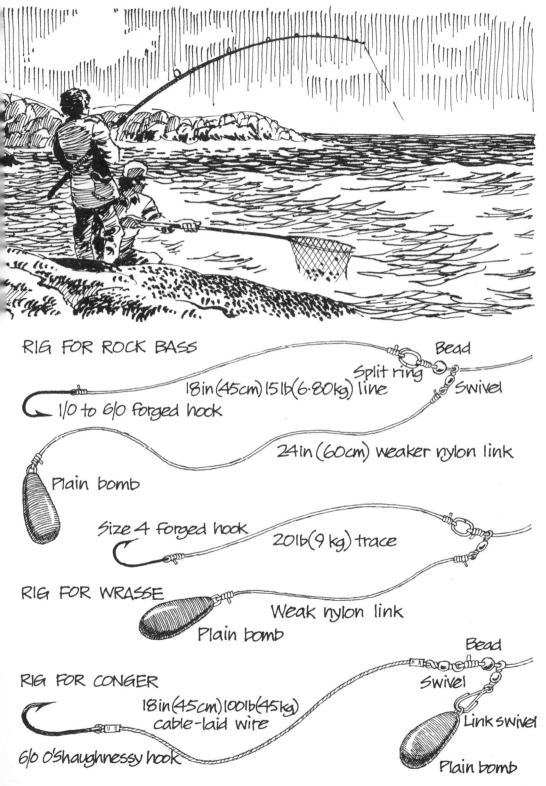

RIG FOR ROCK BASS

Bead

Split ring

18in (45cm) 15lb (6·80kg) line

Swivel

1/0 to 6/0 forged hook

24in (60cm) weaker nylon link

Plain bomb

Size 4 forged hook

20lb (9 kg) trace

RIG FOR WRASSE

Weak nylon link

Plain bomb

Bead

RIG FOR CONGER

Swivel

18in (45cm) 100lb (45kg)
cable-laid wire

Link swivel

6/0 O'shaughnessy hook

Plain bomb

Float fishing is an ideal way of presenting a bait over a rock-littered bottom. Bass, wrasse and pollack respond well to this method.

FLOAT RIG

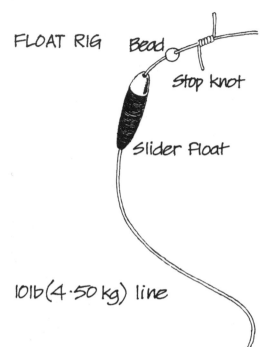

Bead

Stop knot

Slider float

10lb (4.50 kg) line

Drilled bullet

Swivel

15lb (6.80kg) trace

Size 2-4 forged hook

SLIDING STOP KNOT

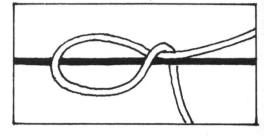

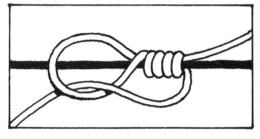

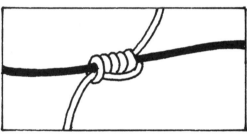

The tag ends of the knot should be trimmed to leave approximately ½ in (12.7mm).

Bass

It is really surprising just how close in bass will be found when they are feeding around rocks. It is always an advantage if the angler is able to survey the proposed fishing spot during the low tide period in order to make a mental map of the area before it is covered by water.

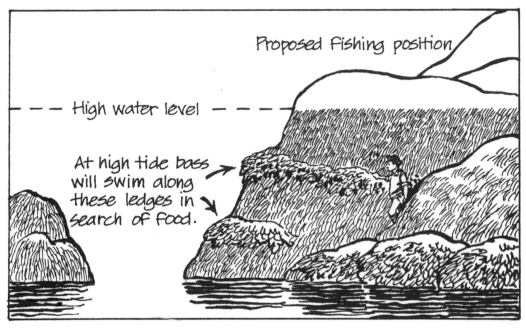

Proposed fishing position

High water level

At high tide bass will swim along these ledges in search of food.

Fish a float-fished bait over a ledge.

Rock bass will take a variety of float-fished baits such as peeler crab, ragworm, prawn or sandeel, but my favourite big-bass bait, especially in the proximity of a harbour, is the head of a mackerel.

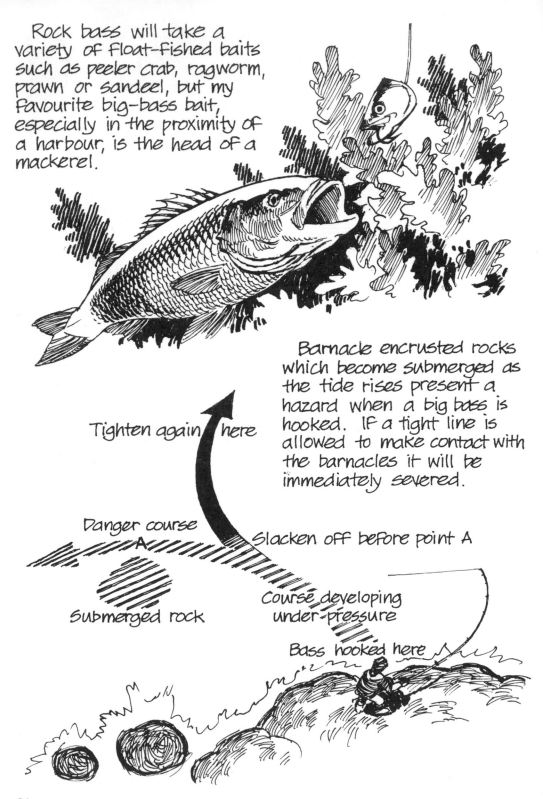

Barnacle encrusted rocks which become submerged as the tide rises present a hazard when a big bass is hooked. If a tight line is allowed to make contact with the barnacles it will be immediately severed.

Tighten again here

Danger course

Slacken off before point A

Submerged rock

Course developing under-pressure

Bass hooked here

Ballan wrasse

Although ballan wrasse can be caught on sliding float tackle, the best specimens are usually taken on bottom rigs. These larger fish live in deep, kelp-filled gullies.

Casting out to gullies is a chancy business. It is far better to select a fishing position which has a good depth of water at low tide and to fish virtually under the rod tip.

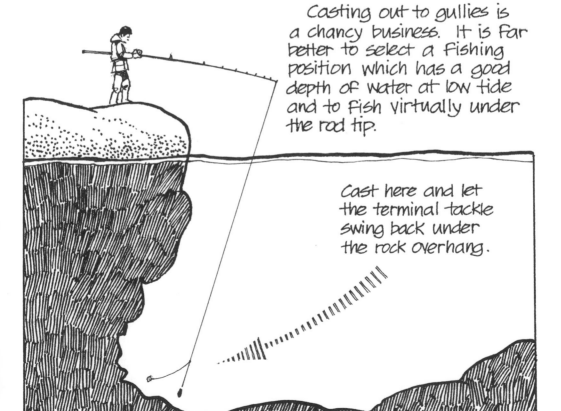

Cast here and let the terminal tackle swing back under the rock overhang.

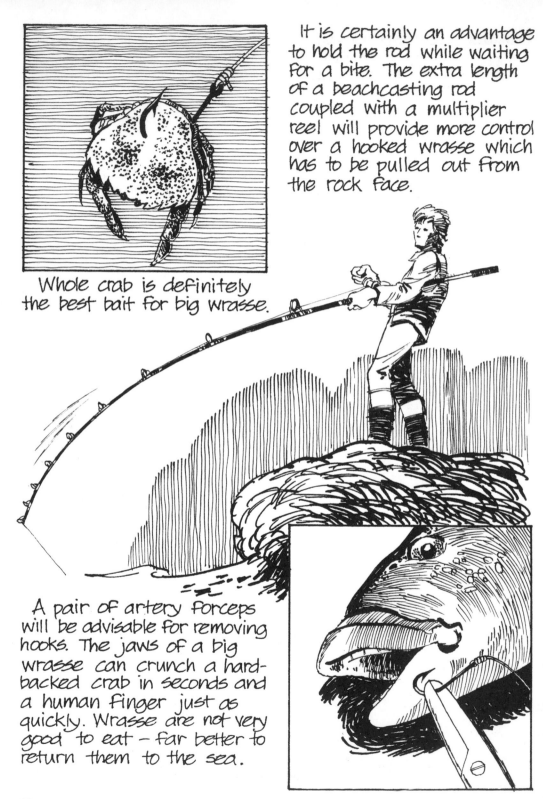

It is certainly an advantage to hold the rod while waiting for a bite. The extra length of a beachcasting rod coupled with a multiplier reel will provide more control over a hooked wrasse which has to be pulled out from the rock face.

Whole crab is definitely the best bait for big wrasse.

A pair of artery forceps will be advisable for removing hooks. The jaws of a big wrasse can crunch a hard-backed crab in seconds and a human finger just as quickly. Wrasse are not very good to eat – far better to return them to the sea.

Pollack also respond well to a float-fished bait. Set the float to fish the bait just clear of underwater rocks, cast out, and retrieve the tackle by slowly turning the reel handle.

Pollack

A belly sliver of mackerel or a ragworm are the most effective baits for this sort of fishing.

A long-handled landing net is essential when landing large fish from rocks. Having a fishing companion present will make the landing operation much easier.

Conger

Wherever there are rocks there will be conger, especially if the rocks lie close to the entrance of a harbour. During the day conger tend to stay in their lairs, but during darkness they emerge and hunt for food. Therefore it is at night that the angler will stand the best chance of catching these eels. As they hunt mainly by scent, a fish bait will be most effective.

Cast the bait on to a clean area of sand, if one exists, close to rocks. Leave the reel in the free-spool position and engage the ratchet.

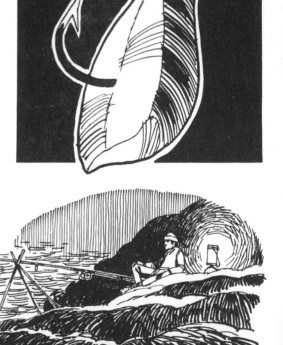

Bass

Bottom fishing for bass is best carried out in an area where fingers of rock exist, with sandy areas between.

The rod should be held whilst waiting for a bite. A fixed-spool or a multiplier reel are equally effective for this relatively close-in type of fishing. Ideal bait will be peeler crab, but during the autumn, when larger bass make an appearance, a dead pouting or mackerel bait will be effective. Cast the bait to lie alongside a rock finger.

Fishing an estuary

The beachcasting rod is well suited to fishing the waters of estuaries where long casts are often necessary.

A study of the estuary at low tide will reveal valuable features, such as the course of the main river channel or channels, the character of the bottom, and the type of creatures living thereon.

The average estuary will usually support colonies of lugworm in the mud just above low water mark, and crabs under weed-covered rocks. King ragworm might well exist if the foreshore is the right mixture of shale and mud. Smaller ragworms will probably be present on most venues.

This low-tide study provides the opportunity to collect these creatures for use as bait—peeler crabs are the bait par-excellence for most estuaries.

Professional bait diggers lay down lengths of drainage pipe or other objects to attract the moulting crabs. Such areas should be avoided, for to take advantage of them could result in an irate verbal onslaught from the bait digger.

Although bass can be caught on leger or paternoster rigs in most estuaries, the humble flounder seems to have more popularity, especially during the autumn and winter months.

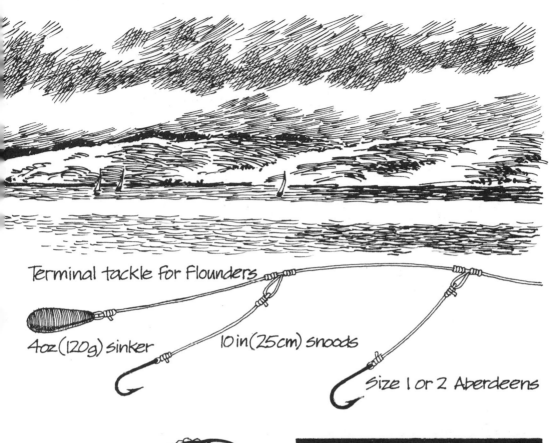

Terminal tackle for Flounders

4oz (120g) sinker

10in (25cm) snoods

Size 1 or 2 Aberdeens

There is no finer flounder bait than a chunk of peeler crab.

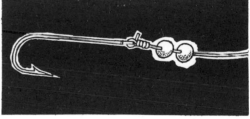

Brightly-coloured beads provide an added attraction, and prompt the flounder to bite more freely.

Valuable fishing time can be saved by having a supply of bait prepared. A flat piece of wood and a razor sharp filleting knife will do the job.

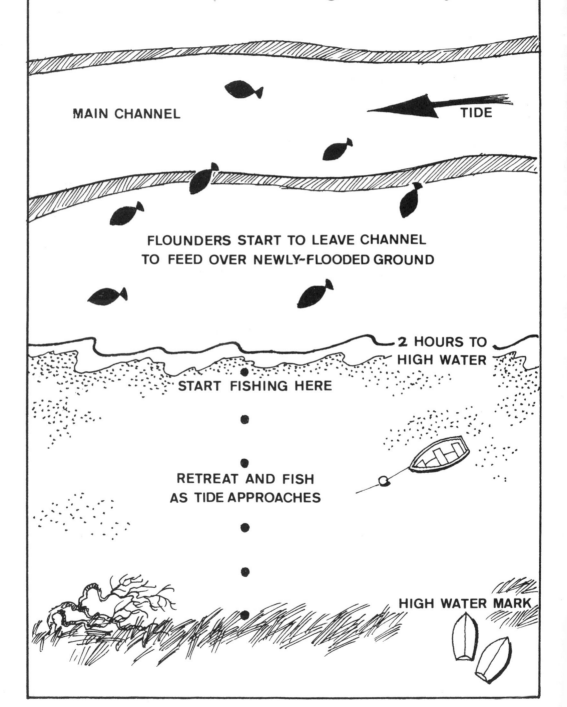

Timetable for fishing an estuary

MAIN CHANNEL

TIDE

FLOUNDERS START TO LEAVE CHANNEL
TO FEED OVER NEWLY-FLOODED GROUND

2 HOURS TO
HIGH WATER

START FISHING HERE

RETREAT AND FISH
AS TIDE APPROACHES

HIGH WATER MARK

As the water creeps up the shoreline the flounders will not be far behind and long casts could be over-shooting the mark. On many occasions a cast of 10yds (9.15m) is enough to get amongst the fish.

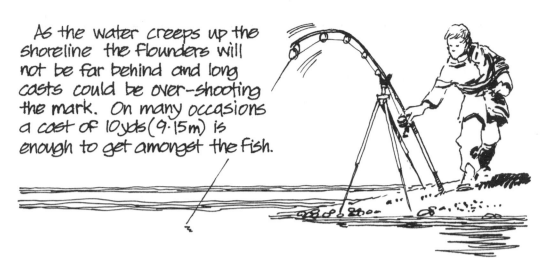

Landing a flounder should pose no problems; they can be beached easily enough.

Sometimes, crabs are a bit thin on the ground, and running out of bait when the flounders are really on the feed can be very frustrating. By cracking open the legs of the crab the bait can be utilized to the full. Three or four legs threaded on to the hook makes a good bait.

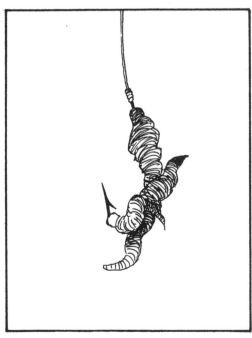

Home-made casting leads

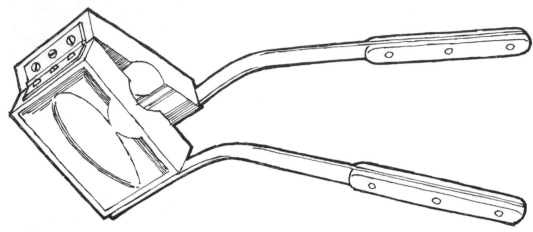

This method of making leads was kindly passed on to me by my friend Russ Symons, of Plymouth.

The advantage of using the converted mould, which is fitted with a hinge and a pair of handles, is that it allows the mould to be manipulated while it is still hot.

Converting the standard aluminium mould is a job for the experienced metal worker or engineer.

Pouring molten lead is a potentially dangerous procedure, if certain rules are not religiously followed, and should only be attempted under adult supervision.

rule 1

Cut the lead into small pieces, place in an old cast iron saucepan which has a pouring lip and heat until the lead is molten. Remove any floating rubbish with an old ladle.

Warm the mould over the heat source to disperse any moisture which may be present.

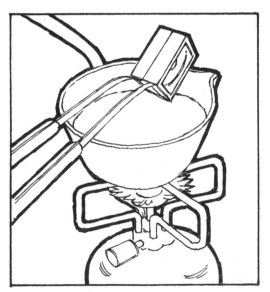

rule 2

Insert the loop, which can be the manufactured brass type with the serrated tag ends, or home-made from 18 guage stainless steel wire. If wire is used, splay the tag ends to achieve a better grip.

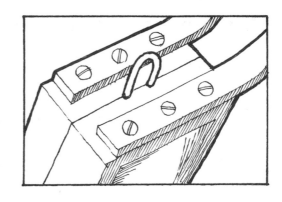

rule 3

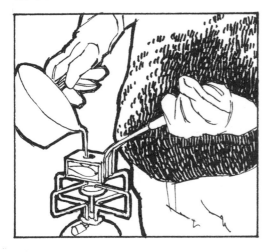

When pouring the lead, always wear heavy duty industrial gauntlets or gloves. Wear thick clothing, making sure that the arms are covered, and safety glasses goggles, or a full-face mask. Pour the lead very carefully, then replace the saucepan on the heater in readiness for the next pouring.

rule 4

Allow a few moments for the lead to solidify, then open the mould and give it a gentle tap to release the sinker. Insert a new loop and repeat the process while the mould is still hot.

Knots

UNI KNOT

One of the strongest knots in use today. This is an excellent knot for connecting a lead to a shock leader.

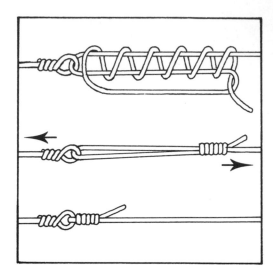

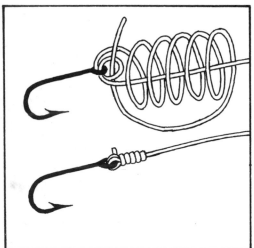

CLINCHED HALF-BLOOD KNOT

For joining hooks, swivels and leads to line. Properly tied, this is a safe knot for connecting a sinker to the end of a shock leader.

TUCKED FULL BLOOD KNOT

For joining line of widely-differing thickness. The thinner line must be doubled at the tying end, and taken around the thicker line twice as many times as the thicker line is taken around it.

Accessories

KNIFE

This is an essential piece of equipment for filleting and cutting up fish and crab bait. It should be kept razor-sharp.

TACKLE BOX

For containing small items of tackle in an orderly fashion. Most boxes are made of plastic which is non-corrosive, but the fittings are metal and will need to be treated regularly with water repellant spray and oil.

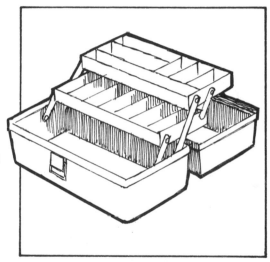

PRESSURE LAMP

There are quite a few different makes available. They all provide a good light, necessary for fishing after dark, and a source of heat for cold fingers.

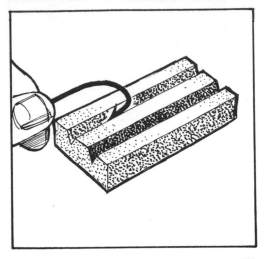

HOOK SHARPENING STONE

When fishing over rough ground, hooks are liable to lose their sharpness. Check the hook before every cast, and if it is blunt use the stone. If the hook is damaged, tie on a new one.

UMBRELLA

This piece of equipment is usually associated with the fresh-water fishing scene, but is just as necessary on a wet and windswept beach, for keeping the angler and his equipment dry.

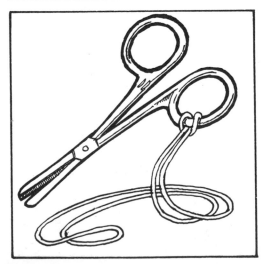

ARTERY FORCEPS

When buying forceps for sea fishing, make sure that they are made from stainless steel. Keep them close at hand for extracting hooks from fish. The best way to do this is to fasten them to a lanyard and hang them around your neck.

Remember!

Salt water causes corrosion to metal surfaces. Reels and rod fittings both contain metal, and both items are expensive. After every fishing session wash rod and reel under cold, fresh water.

Spray reels with water repellant and oil and grease necessary points.

Every so often strip reels down completely and clean the internal mechanism, re-grease and re-assemble. By following this simple procedure your reel will last a lifetime and function efficiently to give trouble-free fishing.